AF716446

Paul Bennett is a Solicitor and Partner at Bennett Briegal LLP a law firm which serves the needs of law firms, solicitors and other professionals. Paul is a specialist in legal regulation and his clients include Judges, leading law firms and individual solicitors. Paul has been involved in a number of the leading cases involving solicitors disciplinary matters and regularly writes and speaks on all things regulation and management.

www.bennettbriegal.co.uk

How to Be a Freelance Solicitor:

A Practical Guide to the SRA-Regulated Freelance Solicitor Model

How to Be a Freelance Solicitor:

A Practical Guide to the SRA-Regulated Freelance Solicitor Model

Paul Bennett LLB (Hons) LLM PG Dip
Bennett Briegal LLP
Solicitor Advocate (All Proceedings)
Legal and business adviser to Solicitors and Law Firms

Law Brief Publishing

Published 2019 by Law Brief Publishing, an imprint of Law Brief Publishing Ltd
30 The Parks
Minehead
Somerset
TA24 8BT

www.lawbriefpublishing.com

Paperback: 978-1-912687-34-3

This book is dedicated to my beautiful wife Sue and our two daughters, Martha and Nancy, who all indulge my writing and talking about law and business issues far too often and this year stayed calm and helpful when I decide to launch a new law firm. Thank you for your love, understanding and patience.

PREFACE

About using this book

This book has been written as a result of around twenty-five years of being either self-employed or running businesses (more recently law firms).

The term gig economy has entered common parlance over the last few years, as has the term side-hustle, and it would be reasonable to declare that my first side-hustle was working on a freelance basis as a DJ in pubs and clubs and later behind the scenes in sports and current affairs radio. This was one of the most enjoyable working periods of my life. From my personal experience in other sectors (you could not be a freelance solicitor back then) there seemed to be common ingredients that the successful freelancer would consistently exhibit. Law is coming to this model somewhat later than many other sectors and therefore I do concentrate on those elements throughout the chapters which follow.

The aim of this book is to give you some tools and some thoughts to help you decide what might work for you of the various tools, resources, tips and techniques that are referred to. Some people will use all of them, some people will use one or two of them and probably most readers will be somewhere in between.

This book is intended as a practical hands-on approach to getting started as a freelance solicitor, but ultimately as in any other sector where freelancers operate:

- you will need to find the work;
- deliver the work; and

- be paid for the work.

If – and only if – you can do this then the model will work for you. As an SRA regulated freelancer nobody can do any of those things for you, so you that must achieve success in each of those three component parts.

What this book is not

This book is not an academically driven textbook or black letter law book.

It has not been written with any kind of student in mind or to help anybody pass an exam or to share any abstract theories. It is purely focussed on helping you start to make decisions about how you might find work, deliver work and be paid for that work within the regulatory regime being established by the SRA.

Why this book was written?

As a lawyer advising other lawyers, I have received an awful lot of enquiries from people who are seeking relatively basic advice which frankly I could not justify charging for. Instead of giving advice therefore I have set out a series of things which might be useful and practical. I anticipate those who are serious will still need to go on and take advice whether it from me or some other source to assist with the bespoke elements of their intended freelance model. This is likely to include drafting a template engagement letter, a set of terms of business and policies and procedures to help comply with the SRA's onerous rules to protect clients.

The Law Society and SRA Materials

In 2019 I was commissioned to write a Practice Note for the Law Society of England & Wales. They gave me their permission to share this fact. The Practice Note is on being a freelance solicitor, I was commissioned to write that when this book was largely already written. Naturally therefore that Practice Note makes use of some of the material which appears in this book. The Law Society though has an established function and cannot share opinion or give information in quite the same way as an author giving their personal thoughts to try and help you, the reader, assess what might be right for you in your own mind.

Similarly, the SRA published helpful guidance, which is clear, in my view, and will assist. But as a statutory regulator there are things that they cannot say or will not say.

I hope this book will act for some people as a complementary resource to those two resources which both the Law Society and the SRA are committed to providing and which I know to be helpful. In my view the Law Society through the Practice Note, a series of podcasts and webinars has excelled itself in supporting potential freelancers on this topic. Those fantastic resources should help – this book just approaches things in a distinct way to provoke the more business linked aspects.

How to use this book

This book has been designed to be used as a tool to assist you in formulating your own thoughts about how the freelance solicitor might work for you or to assist you in concluding if the model is not for you.

You can read it from cover to cover, or you can focus on the elements which are most relevant to your pre-existing skills, knowledge and action plan. I would encourage you to use it practically because doing so should help you because each decision that you think about and research and then address within a business plan is more likely to have a successful outcome. That is not necessarily as a consequence of anything that might be in black and white on the page but it should be a consequence of having provoked your thoughts so that you can apply matters to your own situation or know to seek further assistance, possibly formal advice from an individual qualified to give you that advice, whether that be a legal services regulation lawyer expert in the regime or a business advisor who can help address the business issues.

It is split into three parts:

- Part 1 – Introduction and Business Planning Matters
- Part 2 – The Practical Application of the SRA Rules
- Part 3 – Checklists

I hope you find it useful; I hope you make use of the book and I really hope you go for it and make a success of your future as a freelance solicitor. Good luck!

Paul Bennett
Bennett Briegal LLP
October 2019
www.bennettbriegal.co.uk

ACKNOWLEDGEMENTS

My thanks go – again – to my publishers Tim and Garry, for publishing another book by me and for being helpful, supportive and understanding that sometimes clients come first but trusting me to get there with this important book on the new freedoms for solicitors.

When I first looked at writing a practical guide to the SRA regime a couple of years ago the SRA were helpful, co-operative and kindly confirmed I could use extracts of their published materials provided the source was acknowledged and you will note this is the case yet again in this book as with previous books. If you wish you can always find any source material quoted on their website, www.sra.org.uk.

Two staff members at the SRA were particularly helpful this time around. Chris Handford, Director of Policy was exceptionally welcoming and helpful and shared materials with me prior to publication on key issues to help shape this book. Jatinderpal Loyal, Policy Associate, was a co-speaker at a conference and again was open with insights into the SRA's thinking. These combined insights hopefully help readers as much as they help me.

The Law Society Policy Team have truly excelled themselves in relation to the Freelance Solicitor issue. Opposed to the change in principle once it was approved by the Legal Services Board the materials, the Law Society of England and Wales have created in terms of articles, podcasts, webinars and the Practice Note on Freelance Solicitors which I was commissioned to be the lead author of are an exceptional collection of materials for supporting solicitors with this new means of practicing law. I encourage every reader to access them. My particular thanks go to Robert Cummings, Head of Regulatory Affairs and Economic Crime at The Law Society, and his team including Marzena Lipman Policy Adviser Regulatory Affairs and the now in pastures new

Sarah Brodie formerly Policy Adviser Regulatory Affairs who gave me their insights and time to help address the issues.

Pearl Moses Operational Director of Member Services Development and I discussed the issues at length in a well-received podcast which remains free to access and in a webinar which can be purchased. Again the market intelligence shared by Pearl with me was exceptionally helpful.

Finally, my business partner, Mark Briegal, of the originally named Bennett Briegal LLP has again been understanding of my distraction whilst writing this book.

Each of these deserve a thank you but any errors are mine alone.

CONTENTS

PART ONE

INTRODUCTION AND BUSINESS PLANNING MATTERS

CHAPTER ONE
INTRODUCTION

Law as a business

If you have reached the introduction of this book then it is certain that you at least have an interest in becoming or understanding the freelance solicitor model, which the Solicitors Regulation Authority (SRA) has confirmed it will implement from the 25 November 2019. The model marks a seismic change to the options available for solicitors to offer their services to clients. It is intended to improve access to justice, and it is intended to provide new career opportunities with a lower cost base which ultimately will mean that the costs of accessing legal services may be reduced for clients.

As with any significant change the impact will only be known when pressure tested by commercial reality clients.

The ambitious aim of this book is to give you an overview of the changes and to provoke some thoughts so that you can assess for yourself whether or not the model is – or might be – right for you now or in the future. No book can replace personal legal advice and nothing within the book amounts to any legal advice or specific guidance.

The book does however aim to get you to a point where you can assess whether this business model might be right for you yourself, or if you want to look at other business models which are equally as available under the freedoms being introduced by the Solicitors Regulation Authority (SRA).

The proposals and changes have been controversial. This book does not rehearse those arguments or express a view one way or the other on the rights and wrongs of changing the options available. It simply focusses on:

- business planning issues;
- the SRA expectations and rules in practice;
- some checklists which readers may find helpful.

Readers should ask: is this a viable legal business in my position? The reader will need to think over those issues and make their own decisions. No book can make decisions for you.

The SRA rules need to be understood in context: what the regime is, what are the advantages and disadvantages of the model?

Should you decide this is for you I would encourage you to create a business plan to assess whether or not the model is for you. Why? My belief is that if you can write a business plan for a business, you can assess whether or not that business is something that you want to invest your time and money in.

Ask: Do the rewards justify the risks?

Those are decisions for each and every individual potential freelance solicitor. You will pick up within this book my belief that being a successful freelance solicitor should be business plan driven. For the model to work and to be sustainable in the longer term, you will need to achieve your objectives in that business plan.

CHAPTER TWO
FREELANCE SOLICITORS ARE SOLE TRADERS

The SRA and Law Society materials make very clear that being a freelance solicitor will mean being a sole trader. What does this actually mean? It means that you cannot be a limited company and you cannot be a Limited Liability Partnership (LLP).

You must trade in your own name and a quirk of the SRA rules means that you will not be able to utilise a trading name.

Therefore, if you wish to pursue this model, for example, John Smith a freelance solicitor/SRA-regulated independent solicitor. You will have to identify that you are not attached to a law firm and are not trading through any limited entity.

Outside of law many individuals are sole traders. If you have ever hired a painter and decorator, a plumber or a web designer you may have dealt with an individual who trades in their own name. This means that when the time for payment comes, the payment goes to that sole trader, whether it be John Smith Plumbing or John Smith freelance solicitor. So far, so simple.

The reason though that many individuals choose to trade through limited companies, or as an LLP, particularly in the professions is a balance between risk and reward. As a sole trader if you do something which causes a loss to your clients, and they successfully bring a claim against you, then unless your insurance covers it, your own personal assets are at risk.

Clearly, for John Smith limited, whether he be a plumber or a solicitor, the case is the company is at risk rather than the individual behind it.

The first thing that any potential freelance solicitor has to assess is whether or not this risk is worth the reward that is available, i.e. do the fees that can be earned, and the income derived from this justify the risk of being personally liable? This is a highly personalised decision. You should assess whether or not you are comfortable with that.

Personal liability – Is it really new?

Until the late 1980s it was strictly prohibited for law firms to try and limit their liability and to become a limited company. The Limited Liability Partnership Act 2001 introduced an additional form of business, the LLP, which could thereafter be utilised. The move away from sole trader liability for solicitors is therefore a relatively new phenomenon. However it did happen for a reason. Not everybody was comfortable with taking that risk and for some it was a risk too far. It is very much a personal decision for you to assess whether or not that risk is right for you or not.

If you undertake work in a high-risk area such as conveyancing which is known to be a source of the majority of the legal claims against solicitors then you may conclude that personal liability is not right for you.

The majority of law firms in 2019 have limited their liability in some way shape or form. My own law firm is an LLP with a corporate member i.e. has two levels of protection.

The move to introduce freelance solicitors therefore swims firmly against the tide of the last 30 years in terms of managing personal risks downwards, but there are many law firms who are sole practitioners, or small traditional partnerships under the Partnership Act 1890, who carry the same personal liability risk.

Leading international magic circle firm Slaughter & May remains a traditional partnership, although no doubt their collective resources are significantly greater than any potential freelance solicitor can aspire to on their own.

Similarly Barristers regulated by the Bar Standards Board (BSB) have, until the BSB started to regulate entities, all been traditionally individuals. The barrister model is in effect a sole trader profession as they trade only in their own name. Whilst recent rule changes have relaxed this the take up of entities under the BSB regime remains modest and almost every Barrister in the profession is therefore a sole trader, albeit most choose to work through Chambers, which as we will explore later in the book remains a potential option for freelance solicitors.

What does this mean for you?

You need to assess whether or not you are comfortable being a sole trader.

You need to assess whether or not the type of work that you undertake is high risk?

You also need to assess whether or not the personal liability risk does not sit well with you and your personal assets?

The existence of traditional partnerships, traditional sole practitioners whose firms are regulated by the SRA as a firm and the existence of the model at the Bar make mean on reflection that the risks are seen as acceptable by you. The key question though with this new model is whether or not the watered-down insurance protections offered to freelance solicitors, as opposed to law firms who are subject to the SRA Minimum Terms and Condition of Professional Indemnity Insurance is a theme that time again is raised throughout the book.

You need to assess the impact not just therefore on the risk and reward being a sole trader but also whether or not the revised insurance regime, as offered by the SRA – Regulated Independent Solicitor or Freelance Solicitor model, means that your view is impacted.

The checklist contained in Part 3 may assist you in reviewing this position.

CHAPTER THREE
WHAT IS THE ATTRACTION OF THE GIG ECONOMY? CRY FREEDOM!

Freelancers in other sectors have always been attracted to the ability to be getting paid by a client and for having greater independence over their work.

In recent years the wider economy has demonstrated that flexibility, particularly to work part-time or utilising new technology has had a significant impact on the number of freelancers. Numerous articles have been written about the impact of the financial crisis in 2008 and the economic trends arising since then including a significant upturn in the number of self-employed or freelance workers.

For lawyers being freed from the strictures of partnership, or indeed employment in a traditional law firm, which perhaps is relatively traditional in its outlook, its expectations in terms of hours, and the opportunities for promotion, or working around your family may be relatively limited. A lot of the enquiries I have received about the model start with a discussion such as this: "I am thinking of being a freelance solicitor as I hate my current partners/employer. I dread going into the office and I feel trapped. Can you help me go freelance?"

My answer is always the same: Yes I can help. Let's start with you explaining why this business would work for you.

In the wider economy the freedoms of technology and new methods of working have been transformative, and some solicitors may simply want to access those freedoms. Freelance to employment or partnership with heavy regulation is though an easily transition. As a freelance solicitor your professional obligations will run for many years, so it is a bigger decision that say website design.

The attraction therefore of working for yourself, answering to nobody else, and working when and however you want, is a potentially very strong one but you need to ask if it is a long-term option for you.

Many solicitors in smaller law firms will recognise those character traits although similar looking businesses can be wildly different and stale and stagnated without any of those benefits.

The business decision which you have to determine is does this model work for you and your attractions?

Will your clients share the confidence to instruct you irrespective of where you choose to base yourself? Some lawyers have always worked from home, I can think of a number of QCs who have worked at home for many years but occasionally see solicitors and their clients either in the solicitors' office or in their chambers, which they otherwise rarely visit.

Conclusion

What is the attraction of being freelance to you? Is this a good reason to become freelance: if so why?

The business plan questions arising from that may include:

1. Is the attraction to me unattractive to clients?

2. Is the attraction to me something that will not be sustainable?

3. Will the freedoms and working methods work for my client base?

4. Will being a freelance solicitor give me a commercial advantage over larger firms with more overheads?

Assessing these questions will help you establish whether or not the attractions that you perceive are sustainable and will lead to a viable income moving forward.

As with all of the questions posed in this book there are no right answers and no wrong answers there are only answers which you, yourself, have to come to and decide what is right for you and your clients and potential clients.

CHAPTER FOUR
IS THE FREELANCE SOLICITOR MODEL RIGHT FOR YOUR CLIENTS?

The freelance solicitor model needs to be right for your clients if you are going to have a sustainable income arising from adopting this business model. When looking at the restrictions – in terms of the freelance solicitor status, the insurance position and the fact that with very limited exceptions you will not be able to hold funds on behalf of a client – which are explored in the later chapters the question for your clients is going to be: is my chosen solicitor the right solicitor for this task?

When planning to become a freelance solicitor therefore you need to develop ways of working which not only comply with the more restrictive aspects of the freelance solicitor model but also achieve those freedoms and opportunities which the previous chapter indicated may be available.

If your client base is heavily transactional the freelance solicitor model is going to be more cumbersome for you and your clients. That does mean that it might not be right for you and your clients, because if the legal fees charged to the client are significantly lower than it still may be attractive to clients and provide you with a viable income.

Working without a client account

As a freelance solicitor you will not be able to hold funds in a "Solicitors Client Account". The analysis you have to undertake is whether or not the Third Party Managed Funds (TPMA) solution which is the potential solution to the lack of a client account and enables freelance solicitors and their clients to jointly control money with a FCA registered firm operating the TPMA but the whole process of assessing your business model starts with not only assessing your own aspirations but also your clients' willingness to work in this particular way.

Will your client base be prepared to work this way?

For lawyers who are perhaps advocates or undertaking work areas where very little client money is involved a TPMA is unlikely to be needed the assessment criteria will be slightly different in that it will focus probably more on the insurance factors than the client account factor.

Neither of those barriers are insurmountable but both of those barriers should lead to assessing whether or not your client base, or enough of your client base, to make this financially viable will put up with different working methods, particularly more restrictive working methods. For those that do the freedoms in terms of the model explored elsewhere are clear to see:

- the solicitor the client wants;
- at a fee that is acceptable to the individual solicitor and the client;

- without any of the excess baggage which can come with a traditional law firm such as large offices, supporting other client teams and an excess of resources.

Conclusion

Take the look at the type of work you undertake and assess whether or not the restrictions and opportunities provided by this business model meet with your clients' likely needs and aspirations.

If your needs as a freelance solicitor and your clients' needs as a client of a freelance solicitor merge, or largely merge, then the model is likely to be successful for you.

CHAPTER FIVE
THE BUSINESS PLAN – AN ESSENTIAL GUIDE FOR ANY FREELANCE SOLICITOR

Throughout the first part of this book I have made reference to the business case for being a freelance solicitor for any individuals' future career needs and of course the benefit of their clients. In this chapter I introduce what a business plan is and why it might be a useful addition to your toolbox if you are not already thinking of developing one.

Why have a business plan?

A typical freelance solicitor may be an experienced solicitor of 20 or 30 years standing who has spent many years as partner without perhaps often the need to adopt basic business planning tools. Going freelance though will be different to the experience of being in a larger firm where individuals can find themselves cocooned from the business challenges and cashflow issues which emerge when you are a truly solo practitioner.

Those contacting me consist of solicitors for whom the traditional partnership model has been unappealing for a variety of factors. These have included younger ambitious solicitors for whom the model of "work hard, do as I tell you always, do 15 years here and pay my capital account off so I can leave" is unappealing.

The retiring partner and the "partnership is not for me" solicitor share one common trait: if they operate this model they have to accept they are running a business which must manage its risks and achieve financial goals (even if those are about continuing to run successful to fun a charitable element). This requires execution of a plan to work.

I would encourage each and every person contemplating becoming a freelance solicitor, whether or not they wish to take advantage of grants from business support bodies like a Local Enterprise Partnership (LEP) and the public private hybrids that such support bodies advocate using, whether or not you wish to raise money from the bank to fund premises or the launch of your new venture or if you simply want to minimise the time and the money wasted by acting in an unfocussed manner then a business plan is a good way in my personal experience of achieving that.

What does a good business plan do?

A good business plan will make sure that you are clear about why your clients will want to utilise your services and why your offering will succeed.

It should summarise both for your own benefit and for when you are creating your website, social media and business focused templates, such as marketing material why your business should stand out to its potential clients.

A business plan is therefore about what your business, as a freelance solicitor, needs in terms of equipment, premises and resources. Does your freelance venture need to earn you £40,000, £400,000 or £4,000,000 in year one? How much will your expenses and overheads be? Is this a viable business proposition?

The plan should look at how you expect the business to get to a launch point, to perform over a period of time and the risks that you face as a business and how they will be managed.

It is my suggestion that irrespective of whether or not you are looking to launch your new freelance solicitor business, or you have already launched it that it will help enhance how you manage the potential pitfalls.

A business plan should help you set the direction of your business and communicate your plans to professional colleagues, such as banks, accountants and financial advisors with whom you might want to establish links and also with potential suppliers and clients. Typically, a business plan should consist of the following sections:

- An overview of your business;
- An executive summary of key issues;
- An overview of the market and competition that you face, including identifying your target market and why your offering will succeed in a competitive environment;
- Your sales and marketing strategy, which will typically include why your freelance solicitor position will matter to clients in a positive sense, how you intend to market and how you intend to sell your expertise;
- Practical management of the business including your role, the role of your suppliers (given the prohibition on employees) and the role of advisors (again given the prohibition of employees);
- Operational issues, including what premises and equipment you have available and may need, what suppliers you need to build relationship with (if any), what services may you wish to buy in and any restrictions under the freelance rules;

- Financial forecasting to enable you to see your necessary and likely cashflows, the sales that you need to achieve and the profitability that your venture may have;
- Your launch and early stage financing, including how you will manage during the early periods of the business.

The Template

The template contained with this chapter is certainly not definitive there are a thousand and one different ways, if not more, to write a business plan. I have taken the common themes that I have utilised in businesses in the past, but it is a starting point to get your thoughts captured so that you can execute your business plan.

Complete and adapt the template but treat it as a living document, see guidance below.

The business plan as a living document

A business plan should be a living document given the cashflow projections within it you would certainly want to be managing against these on a month by month basis to ensure that your profitability is enough that you do not run out of money and also that you allow for things such as VAT (if so registered), insurance, unlikely costs such as computer equipment and an online library.

Treat your business plan as a living document and it will help you have a less stressful means of running your business. Formulate it once and don't look at it for 12 months it would have influenced your thoughts and will enhance matters, but you would have lost the optimum potential benefit.

Please make sure that you challenge any assumptions that you rely on.

Remember that it is a tool for you to use and therefore use it despite it not being the only potential option.

BUSINESS PLAN PROPOSED SECTIONS

Section	**Guidance note**
Business overview	This should neatly summarise why your freelance solicitor model would be attractive to clients. You may wish to consider including what background and motives are for setting up the business for noting what legal services you intend to offer. Make sure you explain your plans for the future, particularly focusing on any strengths, weaknesses, opportunities or threats which you, as a freelance solicitor, will face in the first 12 to 24 months of trading.

Executive Summary	You should write this section last. You should draw it out from information contained in the other sections and use it as your working summary to help you, the executive, make your business plan effective.
Market and Competition Overview	Who else is serving your particular market and what do you perceive as your key competition? What are the relevant target markets for you as a freelance solicitor and why may they be open to you, notwithstanding any restrictions placed on you?

	Who are your competitors and what are your competitive advantages and disadvantages in relation to them?
Sales and marketing strategies	How will you attract your client's attention and how will you ensure that they buy from you and not any other legal services provider? Are you going to position yourself in terms of being cheaper on fees as a freelance solicitor? Being more accessible? Being focused on a small number of client needs? How will you balance these advantages against the potential disadvantage of being subjected to less insurance? How will you promote your business in terms of your website, social media through advertising and networking? What are the right channels for you to utilise? In terms of achieving initial clients and sales how will you engage with clients in order to get them to instruct you and how long with this process take?

Practical management of the business, including your role	As a freelance solicitor unable to employ others, how do you intend to manage the business and what support and advisory services may you want to buy in on a self-employed basis? What services being supplied to you will enhance your offering and what will the cost of this be?

Operational issues	What premises, equipment, suppliers and support will you need?
Financial forecasting	In this section outline your expected income and expenditure in financial terms to assess whether or not you have sufficient cashflow to achieve your aims. It may be worth providing a range of forecasts, for example, most likely, optimistic and pessimistic case scenarios.

Your launch and early stage financing	What money will you need to make available to put your plan into action.
Key issues	What are three most important service delivery issues? How do you intend to achieve these?

	What are the three biggest challenges your freelance solicitor business will face? How do you intend to mitigate these challenges so that they have minimal impact on you
Any other issues or factors	How you will address these?

PART TWO

THE PRACTICAL APPLICATION OF THE SRA RULES

CHAPTER SIX
THE SRA STANDARDS AND REGULATIONS 2019 (STARs)

Overview

On 25 November 2019 the SRA will introduce the SRA Standards and Regulations 2019 which can be found on the SRA's own website at the time of writing using the following web address:

https://www.sra.org.uk/solicitors/standards-regulations/

The STARs will replace the SRA Handbook (2011) which will remain in force until that date.

Over the last 10 to 12 years law firms and solicitors have experienced an unparalleled period of, and pace of, change which few, if any other professions, have experienced. There is a lot of change fatigue in the profession n my experience and a healthy degree of scepticism about the SRA and its approach to regulating a profession were high standards are the norm. My personal view is the regulations being introduced for freelance solicitors are too cautious and will change again over the next 3-5 years radically because the aim to trigger innovation will not be entirely met by the approach adopted and set out on the SRA's website. My core reason for this view is that I think the take up and innovation would be greater if freelance solicitors could use a limited company to protect their own assets. Do not be surprised if this happens but the timescale is some years away as the impact of the freelance solicitor model will need to be assessed first and that will take a least a couple of years, probably longer.

This is not a book about the entire STARs regime, it does cover a small aspect of those but my book A Practical Guide to the SRA

Principles, Individual and Law Firm Codes of Conduct 2019: What Every Law Firm Needs to Know which Law Brief Publishing released earlier in 2019 covers those aspects in far more detail. The focus in this book is the rules relating to an SRA–regulated freelance solicitor (freelance solicitor) which come into force alongside the wider SRA Standards and Regulations 2019 on the 25th November 2019.

The SRA's own materials to guide are likely to evolve over the next few months so do not think that complying when you launch will be enough, if using the freelance solicitor model you will need to ensure you remain compliant with any clarifications or changes.

New Model Army

The new model of operating as a freelance solicitor is distinct from traditional forms of legal practice, not least as the individual solicitor is exempt from the SRA Minimum Terms and Conditions of Professional Indemnity Insurance and strictly prohibited from adopting an entity structure such as a partnership, limited liability partnership or a Limited Company.

As a freelance solicitor each freelance will therefore be trading in their own name and will be personally liable in the same way as a sole trader is in any other profession, sector or business. I have used the word "trading" deliberately because it is not how the profession sees itself as "we are professionals" supporting our "clients" and the "rule of law". By contrast by treating law like many other sectors the SRA (and other regulators) are trying to reduce the barriers to improve access to justice. The politics of this are outside this books scope but it is as you should have realised from Part 1 of the book about being a business first and foremost so the risks to "consumers" (in SRA speak) of this approach are minimised. The ethos of the regulators and the profession are not aligned in terms of the terminology or thinking.

This model of practice may be attractive to those with:

- a client base which is personal to them (and hence the clients are less tied to the firm);
- who practice as a freelance advocate; and
- those who undertake advisory focused work (much of which in some fields such as corporate, commercial or employment is non-contentious and highly personal in terms of advising business owners).

The SRA rules for freelance solicitors describe a self-employed solicitor who is:

- practicing on their own and in their own name;
- who does not employ anyone else in connection with the services they provide (unless their practice consists exclusively of non-reserved legal activities when employing others is permitted which is explored below);
- who are not using a trading name or act as a freelance solicitor through a service company or partnership;
- are instructed and engaged directly by the client;
- whose fees are payable directly to the freelance solicitor (because you cannot trade through an intermediary).

Reserved activities and non-reserved activities

The STARs place a significant distinguish between reserved legal activities and non-reserved legal activities.

Reserved legal activities

These terms stem from the Legal Services Act 2007 which at Section 12 defines the reserved legal activities.

In summary these are when not acting in person:

1. the exercise of a right of audience before a court, including the right to call and examine witnesses;

2. conducting litigation

3. reserved instrument activities including preparing any instrument of transfer or charge for the purposes of the Land Registration Act 2002, making an application or lodging a document for registration under that Act; and preparing any other instrument relating to real or personal estate for the purposes of the law of England and Wales or instrument relating to court proceedings in England and Wales;

4. probate activities including preparing any grant of probate;

5. notarial activities so the acts of a Notary Public;

6. the administration of oaths.

The rules for each are subtly different and those adopting the freelance solicitor model will need to understand the impact of these differences and be capable to explaining any limitations in practice to their clients.

Purely non-reserved legal activities practice

A freelance solicitor who only provides non-reserved legal activities as defined by the Legal Services Act 2007 Section 12 and Schedule 2 of the Act will not need to register their practice as a freelance solicitor with the SRA. They may still choose to do so, if they wish to ensure their clients have access to the SRA Compensation Fund and wish to reassure their clients that they hold Professional Indemnity Insurance.

Providing reserved legal activities as a freelance solicitor

Freelance solicitor providing any reserved legal activities will need to comply with the SRA Authorisation of Individuals Regulations 2019 Regulation 10.2 which reads as follows:

> "If you otherwise would be, you will not be regarded as acting as a sole practitioner and you will not therefore need to be authorised as a recognised sole practice if:
>
> a) your practice consists entirely of carrying on activities which are not reserved legal activities; or
>
> b) any reserved legal activities you carry on are provided through an authorised body or an authorised non-SRA firm, or in circumstances in which you:
>
> i. have practised as a solicitor or an REL for a minimum of three years since admission or registration;
>
> ii. are self-employed and practise in your own name, and not through a trading name or service company;

iii. do not employ anyone in connection with the services that you provide;

iv. are engaged directly by the client with your fees payable directly to you;

v. have a practising address in the UK;

vi. take out and maintain indemnity insurance that provides adequate and appropriate cover in respect of the services that you provide, whether or not they comprise reserved legal activities; and

vii. do not hold client money, save that you may hold money which falls within the category of client money set out in rule 2.1(d) of the SRA Accounts Rules so long as:

   A) any money held for disbursements relates to costs or expenses incurred by you on behalf of your client and for which you are liable; and

   B) you have informed your client in advance of where and how the money will be held,

and you choose for your practice not to be authorised as a recognised sole practice."

<u>Why do reserved and non-reserved legal activities matter to you?</u>

It is important for freelance solicitors (and those contemplating becoming a freelance solicitor) to assess whether or not their work is reserved legal activity or non-reserved legal activities exclusively because the STARs restrict how the freelance solicitor can offer and deliver their services.

The media myth of deregulation of freelance solicitors is just that, a myth. The regulations differ so this is not deregulation. Your reputation, your professional standing and your future career could all be impacted by failing to heed the distinction if you are a freelance solicitor doing non-reserved legal activities only and then undertaking a reserved activity without complying with the STARs rules.

Here are some clarifications.

A freelance solicitor is <u>not</u> a consultant, or a self-employed professional attached to a law firm

Regulation 10.2 (b) of SRA Authorisation of Individuals Regulations 2019 introduces a new model of practice designed for those **<u>genuinely working alone</u>**, so if you are working in partnership, through a firm or with others collectively in some way the freelance solicitor model is not right for you and the working method prohibits you acting in this collective manner.

A freelance solicitor should not to be confused with a consultant attached to a law firm or multiple law firms or even with those self-employed solicitors held out as partners in a dispersed law firm model whereby centralised authorisation of the firm occurs and the individual practises under the name of that firm.

Freelance solicitors are by contrast to the collective self-employment models are those who are genuinely self-employed on terms which comply with Regulation 10.2(b).

The SRA Principles 2019

The core duties of a being a solicitor are not impacted by adopting the freelance solicitor model. All solicitors, including freelance solicitors, are obliged to comply with the SRA Principles 2019.

The STARs introduce a revised set of principles which set out the fundamental and ethical behaviour expectations of the SRA. A freelance solicitor is bound by the principles in the same way as any other solicitor and must comply with the mandatory principles at all times. The explanation some of my clients have found helpful is that freelance solicitors are like instant coffee, easy to make into a drinkable coffee by adding the coffee powder to hot water. By contrast the act of grinding coffee beans, filling the filter machine and filtering those freshly ground beans will create a coffee. It will have taken longer, will cost more and is a different format of the same drink.

Which coffee do you prefer? Its personal taste, budget and there is no right or wrong answer.

The SRA Principles 2019 are as follows:

> "You act:
>
> 1. in a way that upholds the constitutional principle of the rule of law, and the proper administration of justice.
>
> 2. in a way that upholds public trust and confidence in the solicitors' profession and in the legal services provided by authorised persons.
>
> 3. with independence.

4. with honesty.

5. with integrity.

6. in a way that encourages equality, diversity and inclusion.

7. in the best interest of each client."

In situations where the principles come into conflict you must comply with those that safeguard the wider public interest (such as the rule of law, and public confidence and the trustworthiness of the solicitors profession or a safe and an effective market for regulated legal services) over those obligations to an individual client's interest. In such circumstances, you should usually inform your client of the circumstances in which your duties to the court or other public interest professional obligations outweigh your duties to them as an individual client.

The SRA have included this expressly in their explanation to the SRA Principles 2019 and therefore you should record any reasoning applied when dealing with the Principles particularly when they potentially conflict and also record, in writing, any guidance on this given to an individual client.

SRA Code of Conduct for Solicitors, RELs and RFLs

A freelance Solicitor is obliged in exactly the same way as any other form of solicitor to comply with the STARs. As with every other solicitor, freelance solicitors should apply their judgment in meeting their own professional obligations. The core duties of a Solicitor are not impacted by this new business model. All solicitors, including freelance solicitors, are obliged to comply with each and every applying professional duty.

Record your thinking for the regulators

Each freelance solicitor shall be personally accountable and must act in compliance with the Individual Code which states as follows in the introduction:

> "...[you] must always be prepared to justify your decisions and actions."

It is important therefore for freelance solicitors to keep records of their decisions and actions. Practically this is a variation of the records most probably keep in the majority of law firms to protect the firm from complaints and professional negligence claims. It does mean however that the freelance solicitor must establish their own records when adopting this model.

Prohibition on Client Account

The Individual Code also contains the following specific guidance for freelance solicitors:

> "4.3 You do not personally hold client money save as permitted under Regulation 10.2(2)(vii) of the Authorisation of Individuals Regulations, unless you work in an authorised body, or in an organisation of a kind prescribed under this rule on any terms that may be prescribed accordingly.

This means you cannot hold funds outside of this Standard within the Code (Standard 4.3).

The business model is reflective that misuse of client funds is key is many disciplinary cases. The SRA have adopted a model therefore which should eliminate this risk in the freelance model by strictly prohibiting the holding of client funds in the traditional working methods.

Conflicts of Interest

Further, Standard 6 goes on to include:

> "6.1 you do not act if there is known interest conflict or a significant risk of such a conflict."

It is likely that there is greater scope for an own interest conflict arising, or the impression of a significant risk of such a conflict arising, given that freelance solicitors are subject to:

- restrictions on how they can handle money (not holding client funds to order and similar);
- some practising restrictions (such as not employing others if they undertake reserved legal activities);
- a different Professional Indemnity Insurance regime;
- the need to explain matters clearly and unequivocally to clients (including potentially vulnerable clients) and to ensure that they fully understand matters;

Do your clients understand your status and its impact on their affairs/case?

As such those contemplating becoming a freelance solicitor will want to make sure that they can demonstrate the efforts to meet obligation 6.1 by recording the risks assessed with each client. The Individual Code guides as follows:

> "8.10 You ensure that clients understand whether and how the services you provide are regulated. This includes:

(a) explaining which activities will be carried out by you, as an authorised person;

(b) explaining which services provided by you, your business or employer, and any separate business are regulated by an approved regulator; and

(c) ensuring that you do not represent any business or employer which is not authorised by the SRA, including any separate business, as being regulated by the SRA.

8.11 You ensure that clients understand the regulatory protections available to them."

As a minimum you should provide this information to clients in your engagement letter and within your terms of business (if in a separate document). You may then also wish to remind clients of those issues in context in any initial letter of advice.

Vulnerable Clients

If the client is vulnerable, for example, English is not a first language or they have learning difficulties, has a disability or whose understanding may be affected by age (due to being a child or elderly) you should expressly record on your file how you ensured compliance with these standards.

CHAPTER SEVEN
THE SRA PROCESS TO BECOME A FREELANCE SOLICITOR AND PRACTICE LIMITATIONS

The SRA Process

The freelance solicitor model requires notification to the SRA of the intention to operate in this way in advance of doing so. This is likely to be a "Notification Form" but at the time of writing the SRA have yet to publish it so it could be a simple email. In adopting the working method of being a freelance solicitor you are confirming as follows:

a) you have practised as a solicitor for a minimum of three years since admission (unless you provide solely non-reserved legal activities as defined elsewhere in this book) ;

b) you are self-employed and will practise in your own name (and thus not through a trading name or service company);

c) you do not employ anyone in connection with the services that you provide (unless you provide solely non-reserved legal activities as defined elsewhere in this book);

d) you are instructed by and engaged directly by the client;

e) the client pays their legal fees linked to their matter directly to you;

f) you have a practising address in the UK;

g) you obtain and maintain throughout your trading period indemnity insurance that provides adequate and appropriate cover in respect of the legal and any auxiliary services that you provide or have provided that takes into account any alternative arrangements you or your clients may make.

h) you only hold client money if it is for payments on account of costs and disbursements that you have not yet billed where:

    a) any money held for disbursements relates to costs and expenses incurred by you on behalf of your client and for which you are liable, and

    b) you have told the client in advance where and how that money will be held.

    c) if your client needs to pay, or is due to receive, other types of client money (for example, damages or money from an estate) then you will not hold it.[1]

If you are considering becoming a freelance solicitor you should allow sufficient time for the notice of commencement of trading as freelance solicitor to be lodged with the SRA before you commence trading and to ensure the SRA have entered you on the register of freelance solicitor so clients and other professionals liaising with you can verify your status.

---

1 Adapted from the SRA Preparing to become a sole practitioner or an SRA-regulated freelance solicitor guidance published on the 4th July 2019. This is not quoted directly as the author has adapted the material for context and clarity, but the duties are set out in this SRA Guidance.

All solicitors with a practising certificate free from practising conditions will be deemed approved and therefore it is unclear if the SRA will require further information other than that provided on the "Notification Form".

Case Study – Gemma Jones Freelance Solicitor
From the 1st January 2020 a solicitor of 20 years standing with a clean disciplinary record wishes to establish a family law advocacy practice working from home. Gemma secures insurance, creates an engagement letter and terms of business to cover her new status and then notifies the SRA of her new status, practising address and insurance on the 15th December 2019
The SRA record Gemma Jones status on their online register 48 hours after the notice was lodged with a commencement date of the 1st January 2020. Gemma starts to operate from the 1st January 2020 as a freelance solicitor.

SRA Transparency Rules

Freelance solicitors providing reserved legal activities will be subject to the SRA Transparency Rules in relation to publishing;

- costs information;
- details of a complaint's procedure including how and when a complaint can be made to both the Legal Ombudsman and the SRA; and

- will need to inform clients expressly and in a clearly that they will not be covered by professional indemnity insurance subject to the SRA's Minimum Terms and Conditions but that alternative insurance arrangements are in place.

The SRA Transparency Rules are not long, onerous or complex but if you are establishing a website for your freelance solicitor business you will need to include the obligations set out in terms of services covered by price transparency and you will need to ensure the complaints notice is clear in terms of the LeO remit and the SRA jurisdiction.

Money Laundering, Terrorist Financing and Transfer of Funds (Information on the Payer) Regulations 2017 (MLR 2017)

Freelance solicitors have the same obligations as any law firm to register under these regulations and to monitor for money laundering and terrorist funding risks. The regulations require a freelance solicitor who provides legal services to others as a part of any financial or real property transactions to register to comply with the MLR 2017 Regulations.

Under Regulation 8 each freelance solicitor will need to ensure that they have complied with these regulations. The obligations include:

- including having a risk assessment;

- policies and procedures in place;

- controls in force to minimise the risks.

Again it is worth noting that a freelance solicitor is not a "deregulated" solicitor as per the media myth but in fact subject to onerous legal and professional obligations. In the case of MLR 2017 that includes risking prosecution if you fail to comply and in respect of the SRA regime of course disciplinary cases will be brought for any breaches of the STARs.

Employing others

Freelance solicitors cannot employ any other party (unless the freelance solicitor is purely undertaking non-reserved legal services). This means that those undertaking exclusively non-reserved legal activities have an option employ a secretary or paralegal, for example, but by contrast a solicitor undertaking reserved legal activities would be expressly prohibited from having a secretary or paralegal. Those restrictions do not make sense to me, but they are the restrictions and breaching them would place the freelance solicitor in breach of the SRA regime and experience shows even technical breaches lead to disciplinary interest and penalties.

The word "employ" is given its natural meaning and will include contracting with someone else in connection with the services, even if they are not an employee under the Employment Rights Act 1996 section 230(1) which defines the word employees in statute and whose interpretation will be very familiar to employment practitioners up and down the country. The SRA's intention is to restrict the freelance solicitors working methods to those solicitors who are genuinely working alone.

The SRA have clarified this intention by indicating that contracting with third parties to provide administrative support (as opposed to legal services) is permitted so long as that service does not amount to employing others.

Case Study: Permitted
The freelance solicitor takes an office in a serviced office environment where receptionist staff do not work directly for the freelance solicitor but do meet and greet clients arriving for appointments. This would be permitted.
Case Study: Prohibited
The freelance solicitor is becoming very busy and successful and thinks about employing either secretary or paralegal to work directly with them and for them to enable them to take on more work. This is prohibited. In this scenario the freelance solicitor would need to apply and become authorised as a law firm entity before employing anyone.

Purely non-reserved legal activities

By contrast if the work you undertake is all non-reserved legal activities then you are free to employ others. However this exemption will need careful monitoring in order to demonstrate that none of the work you undertake amounts to any reserved legal activities.

If reserved legal work arises you will need to decline to act or to cease to be an employer before taking on such work (which may be impractical given the circumstances and your legal obligations as an employer). Anyone who is an employer will need to be aware of the work they are permitted to do and of their duties as an employer.

Holding client money

Freelance solicitors are not permitted to operate a Client Account under the SRA Accounts Rules 2019 or hold client funds (as defined by Rule 2.1 of the SRA Accounts Rules 2019) directly unless those funds are on account of the freelance solicitors own fees or are a disbursement payable by the freelance solicitor on the client's behalf. In practical terms this means that:

a) Any money held for disbursements must relate to costs and expenses incurred by you as a freelance solicitor on behalf of your client and for which you are personally liable, and you can demonstrate that liability to the SRA if necessary (perhaps through time recording records, fee notes, counsels fee notes etc); and

b) The client is informed in advance where and how that money will be held. My view which was pick up and endorsed by the Law Society in the Practice Note on Freelance Solicitors on which I was commissioned as the lead author articulated my opinion that you should give this notification to the client in writing and ideally that it would be an electronic notification (this is because IT records and data shall then record the exact time and date of the provision of that information to protect the freelance solicitor); and

c) If the freelance solicitor's client either needs to pay, or is due to receive any other type of client money such as damages or money from an estate, then the freelance solicitor cannot hold it and the freelance solicitor will need to make other arrangements which safeguards the client's funds which may include the funds being paid through a third party managed account (TPMA) or being held by the client themselves.

Case Study: Notice to client of were funds for fees will be held
An email is sent to Mr & Mrs Moan on the 1st January 2020 at 0926 hours about funds needed the solicitor's own fees and counsels fees for a hearing to occur on the 14th January 2020 at Telford County Court. The email reads: "As you will recall I am a freelance solicitor and therefore not attached to any law firm and my services are being provided direct to you both under the terms set out in my engagement letter dated 1st December 2019. You should therefore recall that my professional rules therefore restrict how I can hold funds and the purposes to which those funds can be applied. From you I need the following funds no later than 4pm on the 7th January 2019 if I am to act in your matter. In your case that means I need from you: • £750 plus VAT for my own agreed fixed fees ahead of the hearing (payable so that I can prepare the brief to counsel and submit a witness statement to court for you both); • £1500 plus VAT Counsel Miss Clown who will act at the hearing (the fee becomes payable on the 10th January even if the hearing is cancelled or adjourned). Therefore the total of £2250 plus VAT (a total of £ 2 925) will be held in my bank account with account number 12345678 sort code 66-66-66 with the Shropshire Building Society under my name (A P Smith). The purpose of the funds is to pay my own fees and those of counsel. This is so that counsel will attend at the hearing because

Miss Clown only accepts instructions when I am in funds and will invoice me within 7 days of the hearing and because I am personally liable to pay the fees due. The funds are non-refundable on or after the 10th January 2020 when the brief fee costs are payable.

Please note the account specified is my business current account and is not a traditional solicitors Client Account because as a freelance solicitor I am not permitted to operate one of those as a freelance solicitor. My Terms of Business detail my status and funding arrangements in more detail.

Please let me know if you have any questions.

Regards

A P Smith

Freelance Solicitor

After losing the hearing Mr and Mrs Moan complain about Miss Clown's costs and performance in court. In the complaint they request their money back and claim this was promised to them to the Legal Ombudsman.

By emailing the client setting out the terms of the funds being requested, the IT records show the reality of the position (the content, the time sent and the email address used). The data is verifiable in a stronger manner than a file letter given the data proves when it was sent.

Further options include the TPMA as outlined above. This next case study shows this.

Case Study: TPMA Transaction
ABC Limited wishes to buy the business of its rival XYZ Limited by way of share acquisition. After 6 months of talks, due diligence and drafting of documents ABC Limited is ready to proceed. As a freelance solicitor you have explained to your client ABC Limited you can not hold client monies or completion funds. You have set up therefore a TPMA with SafeTransfers an FCA regulated payment facility. ABC Limited Finance Director pays in the £10m completion fee and at completion jointly with you the freelance solicitor authorises the release of those funds to Mills and Boon LLP the solicitors for XYZ Limited.
TPMA rules mean that at least one third party control the release of funds jointly. This could be either the buyer or the seller.
Outcome: the freelance solicitor can undertake transactional work by adopting the TPMA working method for funds to be jointly held and thus comply the SRA restrictions on not operating a Client Account or holding funds except for your own fees and payment that you must make on behalf of the client. Alternatively the parties could have transferred the funds direct without the freelance solicitors' involvement, but this could be deemed more high risk and you would need to show the working method adopted was in the client's best interests (i.e. not yours as a freelance solicitor).

Any freelance solicitor (or established law firm) considering the use of a TPMA should read the relevant SRA Ethics Guidance note on these which is a useful overview and should explore the range of providers to see which is right for them (if any). A TPMA does represent a new working method but it reduces the risks of Client Account issues and may for those with limited accounts resources even in firms make sense but for freelance solicitors represents the closest working method possible to traditional practice, albeit with a agreed third party having a fundamental role which does not happen with a traditional solicitors Client Account.

High risk practice areas

Certain areas of practice are likely to be higher risk to freelance solicitors given the limitation on the use of funds outlined above.

Areas which are transactional in nature: commercial property and corporate work, for example, may be more difficult to undertake given the absence of a Client Account when using the freelance solicitor model. The fast-moving nature of residential conveyancing matters and the third-party account nature of the transactions may make conveyancing more stressful for practitioners.

Those seeking to undertake work where holding client money is central to the practice may wish to consider the practicality of a TPMA and balance this against any other factors in relation to different ways of working, such as through an SRA-regulated firm. Transactional work that may be linked to undertakings given in the ordinary course of business and the provisions of funds to order will face a layer of extra complexity. Those are not barriers, but they are hurdles which each freelance solicitor needs to assess for themselves.

Ask yourself: can my working methods be amended to comply with the restrictions?

CHAPTER EIGHT
REGULATORY REQUIREMENTS

Insurance 1: Freelance solicitor undertaking non-reserved legal activities only.

The STARs permit those undertaking non-reserved legal activities to provide services direct to clients without the need for any professional indemnity insurance when the entirety of the freelance solicitor's service are unreserved activities. My view is this position is incredibly dangerous and is a risk to both the freelance solicitor undertaking non-reserved legal activities (because of the personal liability nature of the model) and to clients whose interested are not protected by the absence of insurance.

To place matters in context would you wish to buy electrical services from an uninsured or uninsured electrician? Would you wish to obtain financial advice from an uninsured adviser? You cannot lawfully do this as all advisers need insurance.

Although not compulsory, it is likely in the best interests of the freelance solicitor to obtain insurance which is appropriate and sufficient to protect you and your personal assets when you are providing exclusively unreserved legal services. In the absence of insurance, direct personal liability would exist so your home, savings, future income etc. would all be at risk. As a solicitor starting out you may have few assets but hopefully in 20-years' time the position will be different, a claim 20-years from now after a latent error comes to light is likely to be actionable as the negligence alleged was unknown. The SRA's approach to this uninsured issue simply does not make sense to me.

It is also in the client's interest for freelance solicitors to have insurance and not to have to seek to rely upon their personal assets should a claim be made.

Any reader thinking of using this exemption to reduce start-up costs must be undertaking exclusively non-reserved legal activities and confront the reality that they are self-insuring utilising their own assets. In my view this may place a strain on the solicitor client relationship and is an unnecessary financial risk which can be mitigated by the provision of insurance, even though it is not a regulatory obligation.

Insurance 2: Freelance solicitor providing reserved legal activities

In contrast to the non-reserved legal activities position above, a freelance solicitor undertaking any aspect of reserved legal activities must obtain what the SRA has referred to as "adequate and appropriate" professional indemnity insurance cover in respect of the services they are providing or have provided (including *both* reserved *and* unreserved legal services). The SRA have published Guidance on this issue on the 12th September 2019[1].

The issues to consider when considering the level of insurance may include the following:

- evidence that you have made a reasonable and rational assessment of the appropriate level and wider terms and conditions of professional indemnity insurance cover required for your type of freelance solicitor practice;
- an assessment of the client profile of your work;

1 https://www.sra.org.uk/solicitors/guidance/ethics-guidance/adequate-and-appropriate-indemnity-insurance/

- the number, type, value and frequency of client engagements;
- an assessment of the probable maximum loss for each type of work undertaken;
- any claims history you may have in terms of professional indemnity claims (and I would suggest complaints to LeO which could assist you in assessing the risks you will face due to the personal liability status);
- consider if you need to acquire additional or "top up" insurance for a particular matter or specific risk;
- the information provided to clients on the limitations of cover, the contrast with other legal advisers and why how the insurance offered meets the client's needs.

These issues are likely to lead to very different considerations in different practice areas and dependent also on the known risks. LeO publish periodic reports on the areas of complaints so that trends can be assessed. Your insurance broker is likely to publish guidance on minimising claims and the areas of common complaint. These are useful tools to help you minimise the risks.

Freelance solicitors need to assess in the context of their own practice:

a) how will they record their decision on the insurance factors outlined above?

b) with their client base how often should they review the issue?

c) how often will they review the level of insurance? Initially, I would suggest at 2,6, 12 and 18 months with 6 months rolling review;

d) how will they explain the insurance matters to clients so that the client informed choices can be evidenced as having made?

e) are the freelance solicitor own interest of wanting the clients instructions/work being put ahead of the client's best interests or needs? Linked to this is how you will record everything you do in the client's best interest?

My suggestion is these issues are considered and recorded in writing. Ideally, a freelance solicitor would seek advice on matters which could be from a business coach, accountant, insurance broker or specialist solicitor to help ensure their approach is credible. Why? If the SRA decide to challenge it then the records and evidence of genuine reviews in writing and with an adviser will assist.

Run Off Cover

A major challenge for existing recognised sole practices and smaller law firms is the obligation to acquire run off cover if the law firm practice is to cease. At present the SRA rules do not expressly address the issue of a freelance solicitor ceasing to trade and run off cover.

In practical terms, prudent former-freelance solicitor should take steps to ensure that they have suitable protections in place until the risk of claims has subsided. This could be a very long time because if the circumstances of alleged negligence do not come to light for many years then the time limit under the Limitation Act 1980 will not start to run and the potential claim could take years to emerge.

You should therefore consider the need to acquire cover on a long-term basis and not simply for the period of independent practice. In you intend to retire from practice as a freelance solicitor in five years' time therefore you may wish to decide how you will plan for cover in your retirement and to discuss the options with your insurer. It may be for example that you would wish to plan to fund a longer period of cover as you retire replicating the run-off cover position of law firms.

The SRA Compensation Fund

The SRA operates a fund for making discretionary grants to people whose money has been stolen, misappropriated or not accounted for by a solicitor for which the solicitor or law firm should have been insured under the SRA's rules but was not.

Clients of Freelance solicitor will have access to the compensation fund, subject to the same process and decision making as clients of law firms.

Access to the SRA Compensation Fund is to be restricted to those clients of freelance solicitors who are undertaking an element of reserved legal activities so that those whose practice is non-reserved legal activities will not be covered. This matters to freelance solicitors because clients may pursue them personally more rigorously once they realise the SRA compensation Fund is unlikely to cover their losses.

Holding money on behalf of clients

Regulation 10.2(b) of the SRA Authorisation of Individual Regulations introduces strict limitations on when a freelance solicitor can hold funds. Each freelance solicitor should consider carefully Solicitors Accounts Rules 2019 Rule 2.1 (d) which reads as follows:

> "Client money is money held or received by you in respect of your fees and any unpaid disbursements if held or received prior to delivery of the bill for the same.

The definition of client money under the STARs regime is restrictive. This limits the circumstances in which a freelance solicitor can hold funds as was set out earlier in this book and is something which you will need to ensure you comply with in terms of each and every transaction which occurs.

Rule 2.2 of the Solicitors Accounts Rules 2019 reads as follows:

> "In circumstances where the only client money you hold or receive falls within rule 2.1(d) above, and:
>
> (a) any money held for disbursements relates to costs or expenses incurred by you on behalf of your client and for which you are liable; and
>
> (b) you do not for any other reason maintain a client account;
>
> you are not required to hold this money in a client account if you have informed your client in advance of where and how the money will be held. Rules 2.3, 2.4, 4.1, 7, 8.1(b) and (c) and 12 do not apply to client money held outside of a client account in accordance with this rule."

You should ensure therefore that your bank records and accounting records demonstrate that the only monies held are fees and disbursements and that these can be evidenced at any and all times.

Your Terms of Business should contain the notice as to where and how the funds received will be held, you should then write expressly on the point because if a client wrongly pays in funds you will be in breach. As the professional in the matter the onus to ensure compliance will lie exclusively with you.

Qualified to Supervise Rule

Under the historical SRA regime in order to be qualified to supervise at a law firm each supervising solicitor is obliged to have held a practicing certificate for a minimum of three years after admission prior to becoming a supervisor this acts as a barrier against newly qualified staff starting an SRA regulated entity. The freelance solicitor's position will be different and those with less than three years practising certificate experience will be permitted to act as a freelance solicitor when undertaking non-reserved legal activities only. Those wishing to offer reserved legal activities will need to have held a practising certificate for three years after admission.

Freelance solicitor will again distinguish between reserved legal services and non-reserved legal services to ensure their position complies with the distinct rules.

Newly qualified solicitors as freelance solicitors

A newly qualified solicitor may set up as an independent solicitor during the three-year period following qualification on the basis of providing only non-reserved legal services. If you are contemplating commencing practice in this way you may wish to assess how you would demonstrate your competency under the Individual Code (Standard 3) if the SRA, LeO or client in a negligence claim challenged your competency.

Things to consider include:

- proving competence in the field of practice being undertaken;

- why it was in the client's best interest to instruct you given your relative lack of experience; and
- the distinction in the rules between those with less than and more than three years practising certificate experience.

Many solicitors qualify with many years prior experience in linked areas or using similar skills could impact on the work which it is appropriate to take on without prejudicing a client's interest. A 15-year career as a paralegal or legal executive prior to becoming a freelance solicitor may impact on your thinking but you need to record your decision making.

Reserved legal activities

In relation to reserved legal activities you must have practiced as a solicitor for a minimum of three years since admission or registration. This is demonstrated by holding a practicing certificate so the actual practice undertaken may be limited in reality, but the threshold is the time the practising certificate has been held not the actual day to day workload.

Communication with Clients

You will need to communicate with clients to explain the meaning of and potential impact of your freelance solicitor status. This should include any restrictions on the non-reserved legal services only option. The onus and expectation is on you as the professional in the solicitor/client relationship to get this across clearly and in a way which is understood by the client.

What does this mean?

You should confirm your regulatory status to the clients before they engage with you. You can do this in the following ways:

a) On your website (or in the absence of any website by way of a leaflet or written documentation);

b) By way of an engagement letter to be signed and returned either physically or electronically to you to confirm that your clients have understood your explanation as to your regulatory position;

c) In your terms of business if not entirely covered by a) and b) above.

d) You should explain to the clients clearly the alternative Professional Indemnity Insurance you have in place together with information about the level of cover it and how it will provide them with sufficient protection.

You must confirm to every client prior to engagement that they are not covered by the SRA Minimum Terms and Conditions of Professional Indemnity Insurance and what this means for them, i.e. that a claim could be rejected which would otherwise be payable under the SRA Minimum Terms and Conditions so the cover that they receive from you as a freelance solicitor may be different and distinct.

You should consider only taking on work that you are comfortable is insured in order to protect your own personal assets given that you are otherwise personally liable.

You should confirm to clients that your status as a freelance solicitor can be confirmed on the SRA's digital register as authorised to provide reserved legal activities (presuming that you are not solely focusing on non-reserved legal activities).

The obligations in terms of complaints handling and signposting are the same as for a firm. I have covered this elsewhere, but it must be part of your communications thinking.

As a freelance solicitor the Provision of Service Regulations 2009 and the Consumers Contract Regulations 2013 which respectively cover insurance disclosures, VAT numbers (if applicable) and cancellation of consumer contracts within a cooling off period for 14 days in a wide variety of circumstances apply.

Conclusion

The regulations are onerous and designed to protect the clients of freelance solicitors and not the professional. The regulators (SRA and Legal Services Board) have put the consumers of legal services first. This means you must be familiar with the regime in place and comfortable with the restrictions, limitations and obligations.

I am expecting to see a variety of professional disciplinary investigations and cases in my day to day workload in months 6 to 36 after launch of the freelance solicitor model. Why? Any data analysis of sole practitioners and smaller firms they have historically made up the majority of the cases brought by the SRA. This new model with its limitations will lead to more such cases if the freelance solicitor is not meticulous in their compliance with the rules. When I was the Chair of the Law Society's Small Firms Division (SFD) at its inception we intended to support smaller firms in a new way, and this has been successful but the level of engagement with smaller firms means the focus from a regulatory perspective remains.

CHAPTER NINE
THE CHAMBERS OPTION

Freelance solicitors do not need to be truly alone, but the options for joint working are akin to being at the independent bar for barristers.

Solicitors thinking about going freelance may wish to consider whether or not coming together with other solicitors who are similarly minded to pursue independent practice in a chambers arrangement as self-employed solicitors may be beneficial.

It may be appropriate to ensure that additional support and expertise is available to manage the risks of independent practice (holidays or sickness) and to reduce the temptation to dabble in linked legal areas when you have limited experience.

<u>How does the Chambers Model work?</u>

Each freelance solicitor is individually regulated and will apply the rules to their own circumstances.

The model is likely to consist of:

- Chambers Ltd an entity which is not regulated by any of the legal regulators which merely offers shared services and facilities to Chambers Members;

- Each Chambers Member entering into an agreement to expressly confirm their freelance solicitor status and to agree to Chambers standards of service;

- A website and Terms of Business making it clear that the contract for legal services is exclusively between the individually regulated professional and the client and that Chambers merely provides services and support.

- A membership fee to cover joining and running costs (which may be annual or annual with a percentage paid for services rendered (i.e. not profit sharing which is prohibited).

No-one would be employed by any individual freelance solicitor but of course the freelance solicitors can access pooled resources which could include:

- Office space
- Meeting rooms
- Library facilities (including online library resources)
- Shared reception facilities
- IT support
- Marketing support
- Chambers website
- Shared typing pool etc.

Any chambers model would of course be free to accept members with different skills, specialisms and both those conducting reserved and non-reserved legal activities.

The SRA View of Chambers

It seems that the SRA are very positive about this option.

In their Guidance note on being a freelance solicitor they give it as example 1:

> "Three solicitors, A, B and C, decide to join together in a chambers. They will be offering specialist advocacy services. They have all been practising for more than three years and decide that they do not wish to have the chambers authorised as a recognised body but that they want to operate as three freelance solicitors.
>
> They set up Chambers Ltd a limited company. Chambers Ltd will not employ A, B or C but has a contract with them to provide support and administration. Chambers Ltd rents the premises from which A, B and C will practise. It employs a clerk and secretary, but no staff that provide legal services.
>
> A, B and C each notify us that they will be practising as a freelance solicitor providing some reserved legal services to the public, giving the practising address as that of the chambers.
>
> A, B and C set up a joint website, but the website makes it clear that the services are provided by each of them as individual solicitors.
>
> They arrange professional indemnity insurance that covers them each individually.
>
> Letters (including client care and engagement letters) go out in the individual name of A, B or C as appropriate and not in the name of Chambers Ltd. Bills are also sent out in their individual names, and costs are payable into accounts held in their

> individual names. They do not hold client money, except payment on account of costs and disbursements for which they are liable. Clients provide consent to share their data with Chambers Ltd for administrative purposes."[1]

For freelance solicitors therefore they can be confident the SRA likes the model and option.

Conclusion

Is there someone you could work with using the Chambers Model to share the burden of practicing alone?

Is there a benefit to you of joining a Chambers in terms of resources and support?

It may be an ideal way of working on your own with support as a freelance solicitor but the need for premises and start-up costs are significant. How the market will develop remains to be seen. Historically few Chambers have existed and whilst these changes appear to make the option more attractive than before because the freelance solicitor restriction on employing staff is so restrictive. How will the market evolve? I think some chambers will emerge, but the fee split may make this model challenging.

1 https://www.sra.org.uk/solicitors/guidance/ethics-guidance/preparing-to-become-a-sole-practitioner-or-an-sra-regulated-independent-solicitor/

CHAPTER TEN
THE THINGS WHICH MAY GET OVERLOOKED!

Introduction

When talking to potential freelance solicitors over the last couple of years whether at conferences, talks or when they are seeking specific advice I have noted a list of things which may get overlooked. Please consider this list and the issues:

Storage of files

Paper or data?

How will you store files in a way that maintains confidentiality and allows access to the files, particularly if you do not have office premises? If working from home how will you preserve confidentiality from your family and your family's visitor's perspective? The SRA routinely impose consideration on home-based law firms including lockable doors, filing cabinets and if storing electronically appropriate encryption.

You should identify how you propose to tackle the issue of information storage and record your thinking in a secure space away from the other data/files so that if those are lost you can demonstrate your approach to client confidentiality protection.

Data Protection

You should consider the appropriate data protection policies and processes to put in place and the arrangements and policies you will need to share with clients.

You must be registered with the Information Commissioners Office (ICO) as a, in effect, sole trader processing personal data, if any of your work involves personal data, i.e. personal contact details, name, address, date of birth, telephone or address etc.

It is likely that every freelance solicitor will be obliged to report and register with the ICO.

UK Practising Address

You should consider what is an appropriate practicing address for your freelance solicitor practice. If you are going to practice from home what does that mean in terms of clients or disgruntled parties potentially turning up at your home address?

Do you wish to use a practice address and if so is that practice address acceptable to the SRA in terms of maintaining confidentiality and avoiding conflicts of interest?

Serviced offices which are rarely used will not be acceptable to the SRA unless arrangements are in place to manage that issue.

Undertakings

A freelance solicitor may give an undertaking in the course of their business and it is a binding professional obligation as in any other form of legal practice. If you can not release funds held to an undertaking because of, for example, the third-party control and safeguard in a TPMA scenario then the question will arise "Why did you give that undertaking and how will you now fulfil it?", the obligation to fulfil will remain in place and serious professional sanction may arise if you fail to discharge the undertaking through fulfilment.

TPMA's are likely to require revised wording for undertakings.

You should ensure you are in a position to comply with any undertakings given.

Complaints

An Independent Solicitor is bound to provide the same complaints handling information to clients including at the time of engagement and in any publicity used pre-engagement. If you have not already read the section elsewhere in the book on complaints handling you may wish to do so.

Personal Liability

As an Independent Solicitor you will be trading with the risk of personal liability. You will be contracting with clients directly and therefore will have personal liability to those clients in the event that your Professional Indemnity Insurance declines to meet any claims or does not cover the risk which arises. You should consider your comfort with personal liability and your ability to manage those risks.

Switching to Traditional Practice

As with any new business model there is a risk that a freelance solicitor contemplating a return to practice in a law firm may find firms reluctant to take them on unless the insurance position is clearly resolved, and future liabilities are addressed. It is a matter that you should consider expressly with any future firm with whom you are contemplating joining.

In the future you may find firms reluctant to employ you or to offer you a partnership position unless you continue to pay for insurance for the period during which you were a freelance solicitor.

Reputation and standing

Freelance solicitors are currently an unknown long-term proposition from a reputation with the public/clients and in terms of the standing in the position. The Law Society's long-term opposition to the model was reflective of the risks of the unknown to professionals.

Having lost a policy debate the Law Society is rightly now are pumping out materials to support potential freelance solicitors through the Practice Note which I was commissioned to write as the lead author, in talks/conferences, podcasts and webinars but the standing of freelance solicitors within the profession is an unknown quantity. Is this something you (and your clients) will be comfortable with during the first year or two until the challenging perceptions are understood fully in practice?

CHAPTER ELEVEN
CONCLUSION

Freedom is a wonderful thing as any truly self-employed person will tell you when things are good. It is a proper challenge at other times.

The SRA-regulated freelance solicitor model is not perfect, and it will evolve I suspect over the next few years and some the challenges will increase, and some will decrease – the regulator rightly is focused on protecting the clients of solicitors and not the solicitor's profession. This irritates and winds up the profession as any discussion of the SRA (and LeO or the LSB) will confirm. Regulation without the respect or co-operation of the profession remains a huge threat to the credibility of the regulators collectively.

The distance between the profession and the regulators does lead to some poor communication, poor decisions and policies but these evolve over time.

Balancing this regulator barrier it is a hugely exciting time to be a solicitor and to have this option will aid many skilled and talented professionals establish a work life balance and a business which the traditional models prohibit with their restrictive insurance and high entry and exit costs.

The freelance model will bite the careless and unwary. Those with a firm view of the benefits of freedom will point to the benefits and those with a firmly negative view of change will cite the occasional horror story to support their opinion.

The aim of this book was to provoke your thoughts and focus you on taking advantage of the freedoms as safely as is practical given the personal liability risk.

As a freelance solicitor you simply need to manage risk: each law firm should be doing this now. As should any barrister in independent practice.

If you need legal advice on the issues outlined my website is below, I wish you every success.

PART THREE

CHECKLISTS

CHECKLIST 1 – FREELANCE SOLICITORS AS SOLE TRADERS

Key issue	Impact on you	How are you managing this issue	Record your reasons for being comfortable with the sole trader risk and how you intend to manage this risk
Freelance solicitors are sole traders and therefore cannot be in a partnership, a limited liability or a limited company.	Your personal assets therefore, including all money and property, are at risk in the event of a successful claim against you which is unsupported by your professional indemnity insurance or if you fail to take out any professional indemnity insurance.	What steps are you taking to minimise the risks you face?	
	How do you feel about taking these risks with your personal assets and liability?	Do you have joint assets with a spouse which may be at risk?	
	Are your Terms of Business robust enough to mitigate this risk?	Have you had these checked by a solicitor? By your insurer?	
	Do your clients understand that they can sue you personally?	How does this impact on your client/solicitor relationship? How do you propose to manage the risks?	
Date of this review:	Date of next review being due:	Signature:	

		What evidence and where is stored of these documents being reviewed and applied to the context of your practice is there?	
How will you pay disbursements?	Is it far the minor exceptions to the SRA restrictions or are a TPMA or are those payments direct?	How would you demonstrate to the SRA and/or Legal Ombudsmen the decisions you have made in relation to disbursement payments are the correct ones, within the rules and are in the best interests of each and every client you act for?	
Date of this review:	Date of next review being due:	Signature:	

CHECKLIST 2 – WORKING WITHOUT A CLIENT ACCOUNT?

Key issue	Impact on you	How are you managing this issue	Record your reasons for being comfortable with risk identified and how you intend to manage this risk (including evidence of SRA Guidance being read and followed)
Do you need to take money on account from your clients?	Can you work in conjunction with counsel and other third parties who are prepared to share the no funds on account risk with you?	If asked to justify the holding of any funds in a non-client account by the SRA how would you demonstrate that each and every penny was properly and legitimately held under the freelance solicitor restrictions?	
	Would a Third-Party Managed Account (TPMA) controlled jointly with the client/another party (such as the other solicitor involved in a transaction under an undertaking) assist your client?	Should you arrange a TPMA? Do you need training on TPMA use? Have you read the SRA Guidance Note on TPMA's? (If so when and where is the evidence of compliance with it to be stored)?	
	Does being able to hold only your own fees and fees you must pay to third parties on a very restricted basis limit what you can do?	If seeking to rely on the narrow exemption to hold funds for your own fees and payments you are obliged to make on behalf of a client are you familiar with the Solicitors Accounts Rules 2019 and the Individual Code limitations?	

7. The number of matters you will handle?		
8. The type of matters that you will handle? (In terms of transitional and litigation limitations if any. For example a litigator may undertake contract claims only or not personal injury work).	What are your core areas of competence?	
9. The value of the matters that you will handle?		
10. The frequency of your likely client engagements and the stresses and strain upon you as an individual without support		
11. An assessment of the probable maximum loss for each type of legal work undertaken?	How will you minimise those probable losses if they arise?	
12. What is your complaints history with the Legal Ombudsman and/or Solicitors Regulation Authority, and does this mean you will turn away particular types or work? Will you need to acquire additional or "top up" insurance for a particular matter or a specific risk?	If so what are those specific types of matters or risks and how will you identify and record these?	

CHECKLIST 3 – IS YOUR PROFESSIONAL INDEMNITY INSURANCE ADEQUATE AND APPROPRIATE INSURANCE?

Issues or challenges	**Your response to the issue or challenge**	**Your evidence to satisfy the SRA/insurers and clients**
1. Who are your clients? (Type of clients and are they vulnerable or sophisticated? Business to business or consumer?		
2. What is your personal claims history like?		
3. What will change in your move from private practice or inhouse practice to becoming a freelance solicitor in terms of your likely client base?		
4. What is an adequate and appropriate level of cover in your view given your client base and the value of the matters undertaken?		
5. If you were to receive a higher value or higher risk transactional piece of work how would you evidence a refresh of the adequate and appropriate assessment?		
6. Do your clients understand that you have less cover than a law firm or SRA regulated body or entity?	How will you be explaining this to them and why it may be appropriate in their case	

13. What information is to be provided on the limitations of insurance and at what stage of the client engagement process will you first raise the issue (it must be prior to them formally instructing you)	Will you put this on your website? In your engagement letter? In your Terms of business? (Importantly: how will you ensure that the client has seen one or all of these?)	
14. How often will you review your insurance position and why is it having considered all of the above appropriate and in the client's best interest to instruct you on the terms on which you are able to secure insurance.		
Date of this review:	Date of next review being due:	Signature:

CHECKLIST 4 – INFORMATION TO CLIENTS

□ Have you notified your status to the SRA? (Do you therefore signpost prospective clients to the SRA clickable logo to verify your status?)

□ Has the SRA recorded your status on the publicly available and searchable database?

□ Do you have a website to enable clients to find out information about you including your status, Terms of Business and Privacy Policy?

□ Do you have leaflet explaining you are a freelance solicitor and what it means for clients?

□ Does your engagement letter cover your status, the absence of a client account and your insurance position?

□ Do you have Terms of Business which cover the essential SRA criteria and adequately protect your personal assets as sole trader?

□ Do you have a Complaints Policy? If do does it explain your clients right to complain to:

  □ The Legal Ombudsman (LeO) for service issues?;

  □ The Solicitors Regulation Authority (SRA) for conduct issues?

  □ You as a freelance solicitor who can address service issues before LeO?

□ Have you registered as a data controller with the Information Commissioners Office (ICO)? If so, have you communicated those details on your website and in the Terms of Business?

Date completed:

Review date (for any changes and at least annually):

Signature:

MORE BOOKS BY LAW BRIEF PUBLISHING

A selection of our other titles available now:-

'Ellis on Credit Hire – Sixth Edition' by Aidan Ellis & Tim Kevan
'Tackling Disclosure in the Criminal Courts – A Practitioner's Guide' by Narita Bahra QC & Don Ramble
'A Practical Guide to TOLATA Claims' by Greg Williams
'Artificial Intelligence – The Practical Legal Issues' by John Buyers
'A Practical Guide to Prison Injury Claims' by Malcolm Johnson
'A Practical Guide to Hackney Carriage Licensing in London' by Stuart Jessop
'A Practical Guide to Advising Clients at the Police Station' by Colin Stephen McKeown-Beaumont
'A Practical Guide to Antisocial Behaviour Injunctions' by Iain Wightwick
'Practical Mediation: A Guide for Mediators, Advocates, Advisers, Lawyers, and Students in Civil, Commercial, Business, Property, Workplace, and Employment Cases' by Jonathan Dingle with John Sephton
'Planning Obligations Demystified: A Practical Guide to Planning Obligations and Section 106 Agreements' by Bob Mc Geady & Meyric Lewis
'A Practical Guide to Crofting Law' by Brian Inkster
'A Practical Guide to Spousal Maintenance' by Liz Cowell
'A Practical Guide to the Law of Domain Names and Cybersquatting' by Andrew Clemson
'A Practical Guide to the Law of Gender Pay Gap Reporting' by Harini Iyengar
'A Practical Guide to the Rights of Grandparents in Children Proceedings' by Stuart Barlow
'NHS Whistleblowing and the Law' by Joseph England
'Employment Law and the Gig Economy' by Nigel Mackay & Annie Powell
'A Practical Guide to the General Data Protection Regulation (GDPR)' by Keith Markham

‘A Practical Guide to Noise Induced Hearing Loss (NIHL) Claims’ by Andrew Mckie, Ian Skeate, Gareth McAloon

‘An Introduction to Beauty Negligence Claims – A Practical Guide for the Personal Injury Practitioner’ by Greg Almond

‘Intercompany Agreements for Transfer Pricing Compliance’ by Paul Sutton

‘Zen and the Art of Mediation’ by Martin Plowman

‘A Practical Guide to the SRA Principles, Individual and Law Firm Codes of Conduct 2019 – What Every Law Firm Needs to Know’ by Paul Bennett

‘A Practical Guide to Licensing Law for Commercial Property Lawyers’ by Niall McCann & Richard Williams

‘A Practical Guide to Adoption for Family Lawyers’ by Graham Pegg

‘Essential Motor Finance Law for the Busy Practitioner’ by Richard Humphreys

‘A Practical Guide to Industrial Disease Claims’ by Andrew Mckie & Ian Skeate

‘A Practical Guide to the Law of Armed Conflict’ by Jo Morris & Libby Anderson

‘A Practical Guide to Redundancy’ by Philip Hyland

‘A Practical Guide to Vicarious Liability’ by Mariel Irvine

‘A Practical Guide to Claims Arising from Delays in Diagnosing Cancer’ by Bella Webb

‘A Practical Guide to Applications for Landlord’s Consent and Variation of Leases’ by Mark Shelton

‘A Practical Guide to Relief from Sanctions Post-Mitchell and Denton’ by Peter Causton

‘Butler’s Equine Tax Planning: 2nd Edition’ by Julie Butler

‘A Practical Guide to Equity Release for Advisors’ by Paul Sams

‘A Practical Guide to Unlawful Eviction and Harassment’ by Stephanie Lovegrove

‘A Practical Guide to the Law Relating to Food’ by Ian Thomas

‘A Practical Guide to the Ending of Assured Shorthold Tenancies’ by Elizabeth Dwomoh

‘A Practical Guide to Financial Services Claims’ by Chris Hegarty

‘The Law of Houses in Multiple Occupation: A Practical Guide to HMO Proceedings’ by Julian Hunt

‘A Practical Guide to Unlawful Eviction and Harassment’ by Stephanie Lovegrove

‘A Practical Guide to Solicitor and Client Costs’ by Robin Dunne
‘A Practical Guide to Wrongful Conception, Wrongful Birth and Wrongful Life Claims’ by Rebecca Greenstreet
‘Occupiers, Highways and Defective Premises Claims: A Practical Guide Post-Jackson – 2nd Edition’ by Andrew Mckie
‘A Practical Guide to Financial Ombudsman Service Claims’ by Adam Temple & Robert Scrivenor
‘A Practical Guide to the Law of Enfranchisement and Lease Extension’ by Paul Sams
‘A Practical Guide to Marketing for Lawyers – 2nd Edition’ by Catherine Bailey & Jennet Ingram
'A Practical Guide to Advising Schools on Employment Law' by Jonathan Holden
'Certificates of Lawful Use and Development: A Guide to Making and Determining Applications' by Bob Mc Geady & Meyric Lewis
'A Practical Guide to the Law of Dilapidations' by Mark Shelton
‘A Guide to Consent in Clinical Negligence Post-Montgomery’ by Lauren Sutherland QC
‘A Practical Guide to Running Housing Disrepair and Cavity Wall Claims: 2nd Edition’ by Andrew Mckie & Ian Skeate
‘A Practical Guide to Digital and Social Media Law for Lawyers’ by Sherree Westell
‘A Practical Guide to Holiday Sickness Claims – 2nd Edition’ by Andrew Mckie & Ian Skeate
‘A Practical Guide to Elderly Law’ by Justin Patten
‘Arguments and Tactics for Personal Injury and Clinical Negligence Claims’ by Dorian Williams
‘A Practical Guide to QOCS and Fundamental Dishonesty’ by James Bentley
‘A Practical Guide to Drone Law’ by Rufus Ballaster, Andrew Firman, Eleanor Clot
‘A Practical Guide to Compliance for Personal Injury Firms Working With Claims Management Companies’ by Paul Bennett
‘A Practical Guide to the Landlord and Tenant Act 1954: Commercial Tenancies’ by Richard Hayes & David Sawtell
‘A Practical Guide to Psychiatric Claims in Personal Injury’ by Liam Ryan
‘A Practical Guide to Dog Law for Owners and Others’ by Andrea Pitt

- 'RTA Allegations of Fraud in a Post-Jackson Era: The Handbook – 2nd Edition' by Andrew Mckie
- 'RTA Personal Injury Claims: A Practical Guide Post-Jackson' by Andrew Mckie
- 'On Experts: CPR35 for Lawyers and Experts' by David Boyle
- 'An Introduction to Personal Injury Law' by David Boyle
- 'A Practical Guide to Claims Arising From Accidents Abroad and Travel Claims' by Andrew Mckie & Ian Skeate
- 'A Practical Guide to Chronic Pain Claims' by Pankaj Madan
- 'A Practical Guide to Claims Arising from Fatal Accidents' by James Patience
- 'A Practical Approach to Clinical Negligence Post-Jackson' by Geoffrey Simpson-Scott
- 'Employers' Liability Claims: A Practical Guide Post-Jackson' by Andrew Mckie
- 'A Practical Guide to Subtle Brain Injury Claims' by Pankaj Madan
- 'A Practical Guide to Costs in Personal Injury Cases' by Matthew Hoe
- 'The No Nonsense Solicitors' Practice: A Guide To Running Your Firm' by Bettina Brueggemann
- 'The Queen's Counsel Lawyer's Omnibus: 20 Years of Cartoons from The Times 1993-2013' by Alex Steuart Williams

These books and more are available to order online direct from the publisher at www.lawbriefpublishing.com, where you can also read free sample chapters. For any queries, contact us on 0844 587 2383 or mail@lawbriefpublishing.com.

Our books are also usually in stock at www.amazon.co.uk with free next day delivery for Prime members, and at good legal bookshops such as Wildy & Sons.

We are regularly launching new books in our series of practical day-to-day practitioners' guides. Visit our website and join our free newsletter to be kept informed and to receive special offers, free chapters, etc.

You can also follow us on Twitter at www.twitter.com/lawbriefpub.

www.ingramcontent.com/pod-product-compliance
Lightning Source LLC
LaVergne TN
LVHW022303200926
848481LV00004B/1203
* 9 7 8 1 9 1 2 6 8 7 3 4 3 *